BROKEN
to *Blessed*

Angela Dawes and Vanessa Sullivan

FriesenPress

Suite 300 - 990 Fort St
Victoria, BC, V8V 3K2
Canada

www.friesenpress.com

ISBN
978-1-5255-1315-2 (Hardcover)
978-1-5255-1316-9 (Paperback)
978-1-5255-1317-6 (eBook)

1. BIOGRAPHY & AUTOBIOGRAPHY, PERSONAL MEMOIRS

Distributed to the trade by The Ingram Book Company

Praise for Broken to Blessed:

"Broken to Blessed is a beautiful journey of self-discovery that will inspire you to see the gifts that are already present in your life now. We all have our challenges, but through her story, Angela shares how she chose to change them into blessings. If you ever felt like you needed to be perfect or the best and no matter what you did you could never measure up, this book is for you. The trials and tribulations that you sometimes have to walk through to find that you already had everything you needed within you. It is a realization of the gifts that are given to you along the way, disguised as problems, are there to help you become the best version of yourself. Sometimes we need contrast to see what is right in front of us. If you are struggling, your prayers have been answered here."

Lisa Lieberman-Wang,

#1 Bestseller Author of F.I.N.E. to FAB, Speaker, Licensed NAP & NLP Practitioner & Trainer, Emotional Breakthrough Expert, www.FINEtoFAB.com

"Broken to Blessed is a testament of the human spirit's resiliency and hope. Angela's truths capture your heart and spirit while empowering you to move from surviving to thriving from your own losses."

Carol A. Kivler, *MS, CSP,*
Mental Health Speaker, Author, Trainer
and Consumer Advocate.

"Broken to Blessed, a young woman's journey as she struggles with insecurities and feelings of self-doubt. She realized she always had inner strength and everything she needed to overcome life's most difficult set backs. Angela is an inspiration to all women, especially young women growing up in the false world of social media, unrealistic physical perfection and life's expectations. Broken to Blessed is a must read!"

Kathy Wakile,
Celebrity Chef and Best Selling Cook Book Author.

Angela Dawes and Vanessa Sullivan

"Now is the time to recreate your life. It is not a task for the faint of heart. Indeed it's a challenge, but Angela will be a shining light in your journey. Beginning as a patient and becoming an expert health practitioner, Angela empowers many to fight against the three "T's": Thoughts, Toxins, and Traumas. As a missionary of health and a Gladiatrix (female Gladiator to better humanity), Angela works side by side with me and has been one of the greatest gifts to me and my family. She is a person with a pure, loving heart that inspires the masses and shows up with joy to serve others. Angela's teachings remind us that life is about taking care of you first, so you can be enough to others; to always work on becoming the next best version of yourself; learning how to forgive, so you can free yourself up to heal; and how to find the gifts through all of life's challenges. These are just some of the teachings Angela shares in her book. Now go slay those negative thoughts and live a life of fulfillment, you deserve it!"

Dr. Roger Sahoury,

Health and Wellness Expert, International Best Selling Author of The Gladiators Guide to Corporate Health and Wealth, International Speaker, Founder of Above and Beyond Holistic Wellness Center, Gladiator Corporate Wellness System and SprintSet Energizing Weight Loss System.

Dedication:

This book is dedicated to those who feel broken, lost, or insecure.

I hope that through my story you find encouragement, purpose, and the inner strength to keep on fighting.

Acknowledgements:

To my husband: you have been my backbone and my shining light!

To my Mom: you are the definition of true strength. You are my inspiration!

To my goofball of a sister: you are a prime example of what a success story truly is!

Angela Dawes and Vanessa Sullivan

Prologue

I started each and every day by repeating, *"Today I will let go of fear, pain, and anger. I will learn how to accept and begin my journey to healing."*

I would write that in my journal and say, "Today's the day. Today's the day I will win this battle once and for all."

Well, that day never came because I continued writing that phrase and fighting my battle for another sixteen tiresome years.

Well, today *is* the day!

And for the first time ever, I relive and tell my story, the raw, real, and uncut version.

Angela Dawes and Vanessa Sullivan

One Body

My journey has been filled with many challenges that left me broken, angry, and questioning my true purpose. I often made excuses, blamed others, and relentlessly asked, "Why me?"

Every day was a constant battle feeling like I had to live my life in the shadows of society.

If I could tell you I had a really dark, horrific childhood, it would be easier to understand how the pressures of society took over my mind and body. If I could tell you my parents pinched my skin calling me fat or bullies in school called me names, it would be easier to understand why this disorder took over. The thing is, none of that happened. I cannot emphasize enough how amazing my friends and family were to me. I was a friend to everyone; an athlete, and I worked hard at everything I put my mind to. My parents loved, supported, and took care of me unconditionally. They were my biggest fans and my best friends.

I leaned on them for guidance and strength throughout different areas of my life, but they were equally important to me. I adored my sister and always looked up to her. Unfortunately, because of the crowd she associated with, she went through a lot of rough teen years. My sister used to be the "troubled child" as I would label it. And when there's a troubled child, there has to be the "perfect" one, to balance it all out. In my parents' eyes, I could do no wrong; I had all the answers and was on the right path to making all my dreams come true. I wasn't off getting into trouble, I was laser-focused on becoming a career woman and being successful. Others often looked up to me because I was the go-getter and never quit. In school I wouldn't accept any grade less than an A. As an athlete, I would personally hold myself responsible for any lost games.

And so it began, the never-ending battle of being anything less than "perfect."

I remember being in middle school and inseparable from my best friend. We both had a sister, our parents were best friends, and we danced and played soccer together; we even took family vacations as a group. We had so much in common, but I often questioned the one thing we didn't: "Why couldn't I look like her?" She was a lot skinnier than I was. I analyzed and compared everything she ate versus what I ate. I became embarrassed to eat in front of her, thinking she was judging everything about me. The hard truth is she never said anything to make me feel that way. All of those insecurities were created inside my head. Those thoughts continued as I went into high school. I played varsity soccer and compared myself to all my teammates thinking, "Why couldn't my legs be skinnier, rather than muscular?" This behavior and mindset was a poison that completely consumed me.

Whether it was with a different friend, or playing a different sport, these thoughts became leeches, gripping onto my mind and sucking all the positivity out of me. The thoughts would get louder, and stronger, more aggressive in my mind. As a young girl, my thoughts were like little flurries or snowflakes, but over the years they snowballed into an avalanche.

At fifteen I joined a gym with my sister and immediately fell in love with fitness. We didn't spend much time together outside of the gym. After all, when you're eighteen who wants to hang out with their younger sister? Working out was the one thing we did together and I always looked forward to those sessions. After some time, I began comparing myself to my sister who had "abs of steel" and could run for hours without gasping for air. What started as sisterly bonding, turned quickly into a competition in my mind. My sister had the confidence to wear a sports bra and show off her stomach, but I lacked that confidence and would cover up. In the gym I would wear long t-shirts and stay covered, but at home or in private I would be fixated on my body and often check to see if there were any noticeable changes.

Although the thoughts in my mind grew darker and darker, my love (or should I say obsession) for fitness grew stronger and stronger. I started working out in-between our sessions in hopes of matching her endurance, strength, and physique. I focused on abdominal exercises, increased my cardio, and lifted weights as heavy as I could. At age fifteen, my body was already completely worn out.

Looking at me from a distance, I had the "perfect" family and "perfect" life. What could be wrong? The thing was, internally everything *was* wrong.

When my friends and I were in high school, we

used to attend many parties and go out dancing. We would come home late at night and often indulge in comfort food. Many nights I would go back to my boyfriend's house and he would make a full course meal: steak, rice, and beans. It all looked and smelled good, but I always felt guilty eating "unhealthy" foods that late at night. I remember being so frustrated because there was never anything healthy in the house. The best I could find, and at that age I actually thought was healthy, was eating raisin bran cereal with skim milk.

My nutrition was "perfect" in front of people. If I was with some friends at the diner, they would get burgers and disco fries, and I would be eating egg whites and spinach. No one ever saw me eat anything bad, but I binged when no one was watching. I was just very good with hiding and being discrete. No one questioned my madness; they even respected my commitment to a healthy lifestyle. *But was it really?*

I never thought I was overweight. I never looked in the mirror and saw an overweight person staring back at me. I was just so afraid of gaining weight that every time I ate something I perceived to be unhealthy, I had the immediate urge to get rid of it. From my appearance alone, one wouldn't suspect I had any body issues. You would think, because I forced myself to throw up so often I would appear frail, but my tank was never on "E", so to speak. I always tried to outsmart this disorder; after I purged I would immediately refill on a small meal or snack. This became a key aspect as to why no one caught on. I thought the only way to know I had lost control of this disorder would be if I appeared weak and frail. As far as I can recall, you couldn't see my bones and I wasn't collapsing from lack of energy. I was able to maintain my normal daily and fitness routines.

There are many different severities of this disorder and mine was one that wasn't physically noticeable. I also wasn't sleeping all the time, or skipping school, practices, or games. Since those were not issues, I didn't understand the damage I was doing. If I had changed my clothes, appearance, and/or people began commenting, then it would be safe to admit I had lost control and hit rock bottom. Truthfully, throughout this period of my life, my weight hadn't fluctuated very much.

In fact, I often received compliments on my body from both guys and girls. Maybe because I always received them, that's what I was afraid of losing. The sad thing was the comments meant nothing to me. I was numb to hearing those compliments because I didn't believe them myself. Something that was so detrimental to my life and resulted in me lying to loved ones, ruining my body, and obsessing over my appearance, when it all paid off by having people acknowledge my body, I didn't even care. I was still so focused on the habit. Working out in the gym I would often hear people say they were going to "start dieting on Monday." Many Mondays came and went and a new year would fast approach, the same resolutions with the same excuses as to why they weren't achieved. The story of my life! Every night I would lie in bed and say to myself, "Today was the last day this will happen." I had the right intentions every night, but in the morning the voices in my head were stronger.

Eventually those voices became too loud and too consistent to drown out, that my habits only progressed. I would bring my own food to holiday parties. My family would joke, "Here's Angela with her Tupperware." Even on a holiday, I would attempt to eat healthy when the reality was that the food looked and smelled so good I would occasionally sneak a bite of something when no one was looking. That would have been okay if that were all it was, but it didn't stop there. My weak points were during the clean up after the party was over. That's when I would binge. *What was I trying to prove?*

Each and every day, my food intake had to be planned out. Even worse, my life was planned around my eating schedule, which was every two-three hours. (Sad, I know.) I would pack snacks when I knew I would be out running errands. Some days I would wait at home watching the clock until it was my next time to eat. That way, I didn't have to pack too many meals with me when I did leave the house. Prepping the night before work took hours. If I worked a twelve-hour shift, that would be six meals I would need to bring with me! I can't stress it enough, my whole life was based off of my eating schedule.

Before attending any social gathering I would analyze the event in my head: what are they going to have to eat? What am I eating before I leave? Should I bring my own food? I would avoid all situations where I had no healthy eating options. No one ever questioned my eating habits or brought the subject up to me. They didn't ask me why I chose the foods

I did, or why I ate before we went out, they just accepted that was part of who I was. And since it never affected my grades, appearance, or sports, there never was a reason to.

Yet food and fitness was all I thought about. It consumed every space in my brain. It was impossible for me to find any purpose or passion in anything else.

Anytime I ate anything I felt so full and disgusted immediately after. You'd be surprised, what I consider to be unhealthy others might not. At my lowest point, even eating egg whites were calories that I didn't want in my body. The scary reality was, I didn't care if what I was eating was considered healthy or not. In my mind, I was simply eating foods that contained calories and calories signified weight gain.

The more calories I consumed, the more concerned I became about gaining weight, so I would go into the bathroom to make myself vomit. It was sporadic after my first time. Sometimes I would go weeks, sometimes only days, before it would happen again and I would find myself in my bathroom, forcing myself to vomit. Unfortunately, once I saw how easy it was to take in the bad and then quickly dispose of it, the behavior became the quickest "fix" I could think of. When I saw how easy it was to purge and how good I felt after, it became second nature. It got to a point where every time I ate something I always felt sick: my stomach was bloated and I had sharp pains. It seemed like I always had digestive issues after I binged and purged, but I never connected the dots.

This disorder took a sharp turn when I was seventeen years old.

I slept over at my boyfriend's house quite often. He had no idea I was bulimic and I tried so hard to keep it that way. Because purging was an automatic reaction after every meal, I had to figure out a way to not get caught.

To avoid any suspicion from being in the bathroom for a few minutes longer than usual, I would turn on the water to make it seem like I was showering. I would make the water scorching hot so the mirrors would immediately fog up. On one particular day, I noticed in the mirror a blurry image was staring back at me. Kind of ironic actually: not recognizing the person staring back at me was a figurative statement *and* a literal one.

A pounding on the door brought me back to reality. My boyfriend asked me if everything was okay and what was taking so long. I stumbled on my response, quickly flushing the toilet.

Within seconds the power I thought I had was immediately stripped.

He barged into the bathroom and there I was hovering over the toilet bowl, tears streaming down my face. Up until this moment I had mastered this double life. I "perfected" it to where no one had ever questioned me before. I thought I was so good at hiding it, but with him now staring at me I felt like a complete failure. We only made eye contact for a split second. Seeing the confusion and concern in his face was too hard for me to process. I couldn't find the answers to any of his questions. I couldn't explain myself.

You might think that his catching me in the act of purging would offer me a starting point to make my life better. Instead, it made everything worse. The competitor in me saw a new challenge, to work harder than ever to avoid getting caught again. Looking back now, I see how much trouble I really was in if that was my thought process.

My life was like shaking a soda can for many years, and one day from the build-up of pressure, it exploded.

My boyfriend gave me an ultimatum: either I tell my parents or he would. I had several chances to confess to them what I had been doing for years, but could never do it. The thought of them thinking anything less of me than their "perfect" little princess was too difficult to bear. I didn't have the courage to tell them my dark secret. I don't blame him for setting up the family meeting; he was scared and concerned and he did what he thought he was supposed to do to help save me. I remember sitting with my parents when he said to them, "Angela has something to tell you." Him and I were sitting on a couch across from my parents and the room was quiet and tense. I didn't hide this disorder because I was concerned about my health or body. I hid it because I was so afraid of their disappointment. What was I even going to tell them now? I couldn't think of anything more than simply saying, "I'm sick." My Mom looked so confused. She asked, "What do you mean, sick?" But I couldn't say the words. To this day I still can't. Ultimately, he looked at my Mom and carefully spoke the words that still make me cringe, "Angela is bulimic." My

Mom instantly broke down crying, blaming herself for not recognizing that her baby was suffering and my poor father didn't know who to console first, or what to even say.

Immediately I was swept away to a psychiatrist. On my first visit the psychiatrist looked at me and said, "You have the *perfect* body, why are you doing this to yourself?" If my eyes could roll further into my head, they would have gotten stuck there forever. This is the same exact line I'd been told for years. If I believed I had the "perfect" body, I *wouldn't* be doing this to myself. A doctor should know that! I believed she couldn't help me if she couldn't even understand me. And if only I understood me, I would have to find a way to recover on my own. That was the last time I stepped foot into a psychiatrist's office.

With my parents having to deal with the stresses of every day life, I could not bare to tell them how I felt or what was truly going on. I would continuously tell myself, "Let Go and Let God." Up until this point I never really had faith. That saying had just popped into my life one day and I never could part ways from it. I had to release some control and remember that God was going to take care of me, but what I could control I would have to handle all on my own.

And I did just that for the next decade, because I could *never* disappoint my parents.

Unfortunately not much had changed for me over those years with my eating disorder. My boyfriend and I parted ways and I was on to the next adventure: college. While I was studying radiology, I became a personal trainer because fitness was a passion of mine. I initially worked out because the hungry athlete in me felt fed whenever I did. Because I didn't play collegiate sports, I was constantly yearning for an opportunity to compete. I became a trainer because I wanted to support others in obtaining optimum health. Truthfully, it had nothing to do with my personal body image, their insecurities, or for anyone to *look* a certain way. It was always about being the best, most healthy version of yourself. I was great at giving advice to others, but had a difficult time applying that advice to my own life.

My boss at the time was a very successful

professional body builder who told me I had the "perfect" body.

Hearing that come from a professional in the industry who was a well-known judge for competitions, and a trainer for creating the "perfect" body gave me desire to start competing. My expectation wasn't to place; it was solely to gain some confidence. I wanted so desperately to be proud of my own body. Where training was about my client, competing was all about me. My attention had to be on me 100% of the time: training twice a day, weighing my food, taking supplements, and simply sacrificing every area of my life.

My trainer would have me eat every two hours. In my mind, I noticed how often I would be eating and that would make me paranoid that I was gaining weight. In reality, if one is eating lean protein and vegetables every two hours- weight gain shouldn't be an issue. Even still, I would make myself vomit, even if egg whites were all I had consumed. There was no part of me that believed that food was fuel. I was so tired from making myself sick that sometimes I wouldn't even realize it was happening until I finished. I would look over at my dog lying on the carpet next to me watching me destroy my body. His eyes would plead with me to stop. But I couldn't. So, I laid on the carpet and cried with him.

I remember being backstage at the figure competition as everyone was prepping physically and emotionally for his or her moment to shine. To get their muscles pumped some would use resistance bands, dumbbells, and/or do push-ups. I, on the other hand, stood there staring at these women analyzing and comparing my body to theirs. *Looking back now, how was my pursuit about health?* I would think about all that I had sacrificed physically, emotionally, and financially, all for this one day. I started overanalyzing why I was even there: *why would someone with an eating disorder put herself on stage for the rest of an industry to judge?* I even had to go to an "adult store" to get clear stiletto heels. If I could just walk across the stage in those stiletto shoes I would feel accomplished. I didn't care about what the judges thought; I just had to prove to myself I could do it. I had to prove something to myself and gain a sense of confidence. Apparently, I was more of a competitor than I realized because the second I walked out on stage, I realized I did care about what the judges thought. It was important for me to do well. I had a big crowd there supporting me. I specifically remember pointing out my parents in the audience, not wanting to disappoint them. A reoccurring fear of mine.

Figure competing started out well, but it ended with finding out this wasn't about getting healthy or building confidence. Competing was bringing out unrealistic expectations of myself. The crash dieting and over training led to a sluggish metabolism, missed periods, and bad skin. It was also affecting my social life; I dedicated all my time and energy to this lifestyle, so I couldn't enjoy hanging out with my friends or going out to eat with them. The behaviors that came from this type of lifestyle were detrimental to my already existing unhealthy habits.

I initially wanted to gain confidence from this experience, but ultimately it led to micromanaging every move I made: every time I worked out, ate, and/or weighed in I overanalyzed how to be better than the day before. Instead of gaining confidence, I was putting more pressure on myself to meet a stereotype I had created in my mind. A superficial look of approval for the generation and culture we were currently living in, believing photo-shopped images were a reality and I needed to become them. Quickly the pressures of "perfection" became another consumption of my mind.

I was always trying to justify why I was competing. I claimed to do it because health was my priority, *but was it really?* I claimed to do it to make my parents proud, *but was it really?* I claimed to do it to gain self-confidence, but again *was it really?* I wasn't being healthy, my parents were proud of me with or without the competition, and after competing it only made my insecurities worse.

Word of advice: not everything you hear, see, or read is accurate. I never really understood that until I entered my first figure competition and experienced behind the scenes firsthand. To get fit, and most importantly healthy, is nothing short of hard work, sacrifice, and consistency. After one competition, I realized I couldn't sustain this lifestyle and I stopped competing. I put my body through such torture all for a very short reward. Just because information gets published in a magazine, doesn't mean it's the truth. Health, nutrition, and fitness claims are made every day via the Internet, television, and social media. I personally turned to those sources for motivation and information. I would have done *anything* to look like them.

Because of those expectations I set for myself, I realized this competition had to be my first and last. Especially for me, I had to always remember to stay away from the "get fit quick" traps, and focus on the long term.

I remained a personal trainer for another six years, hoping to balance my disorder with this career. In the end, I had to choose which was more important: following my passion or overcoming and healing my disorder. Eventually I reached a point in my life were I wasn't going to make any more excuses. I wasn't strong enough to fight this disorder being in an environment that fed it.

I constantly battled between being a homebody and loner versus wanting to go out and socialize. Once I went out I immediately regretted it and had anxiety. *'Why did I go out? Why did I wear this outfit? My hair looks so bad compared to that girls'.* I never really drank so I watched while everyone else did. Since there was never anything positive running through my head when I was out, I would try to stay home more often, hoping those thoughts wouldn't continue to consume me. Wishful thinking. I would find myself scrolling through social media and seeing everyone have fun with friends and family and all I can feel was jealousy. I wanted to be out there and have fun. But when I tried… those negative thoughts grew louder. *What's wrong with me?*

One night we were at a bar for my friends' birthday and they asked a random guy to take a picture of us all. I immediately darted from the group and stood behind him, he looked puzzled. "Do you not want to be in the picture?" he asked me. I politely smiled and shook my head. I don't like pictures or the attention.

I thought to myself later, was it really that: me not liking attention? Or was it because I knew what would come of it? I would look at the picture, rip myself apart, and then compare myself to others: overanalyzing first and critiquing myself after. I never did have anything nice to say about myself, only the things I hated.

Because I never liked taking pictures, I have only a few to look back on from my college years. The clothes I wore were anything *but* from an insecure person. Which is senseless to me because sitting here now I can't think of a time in my life where I ever felt confident enough to wear clothes like that. I suppose the take away from that lesson is this: everyone is different; many think the first warning signs of an eating disorder are baggy clothing. I was opposite from that stereotype. Looking back at my college years, I wore the shortest shorts, crop top shirts, and other clothing pieces that showed off one's figure.

If only I could go back in time and shake myself. Grab my own face and look into my eyes and explain that the damage was happening whether I understood it or not. My period was irregular so I was prescribed birth control for the simple reason of regulation. I couldn't even get my cycle naturally, and even then it never occurred to me the harm I was doing to myself. I had consistent sore throats, broken blood vessels on my face, and constant sinus infections from the pressure and strain of vomiting.

I truly didn't understand the damage I was doing. And if you can't understand the damage, why work towards a solution to fix anything?

There was nothing to fix.

Damage and naïveté: two words that went hand in hand for me.

In my late twenties I finally told my best friend, Brigitte, that I had an eating disorder. She was incredibly supportive and inspiring. However, she had never had an idea about my secrets before, and she was my very best friend, the one person who, supposedly, knew everything about me, I hid my disorder from her. How do you tell someone everything? I mean every time I sneezed she knew about it, and I still couldn't come around to telling her one of the most important parts about myself. I wanted her, and everyone, to perceive me as the girl who could do no wrong. I knew she would support and love me through it, but until now that wasn't enough reason to come clean. The secret was eating me inside and I needed to get it out. I also knew she would be the one to consistently stay on me about my recovery and that's why I went to her first.

Even if the people closest to me had known what was going on, I don't think it would have made a difference. They could have tried talking to me about changing my behaviors, but I probably wouldn't have heard them. I was my own worst enemy. Every time

I tried to see the light at the end of the tunnel, the devil on my shoulder would dim it.

> *"Self-love, self-respect, self-worth: There's a reason they all start with 'self.' You can't find them in anyone else." (Unknown)*

Even years later, long after I was married, if I was home alone the thought of binging and purging was constantly there. My emotions would take over and I would pick at food even if I wasn't hungry, and that picking didn't stop. I would find myself yet again in the bathroom making myself vomit. I remember so many times I was about to tell my husband. He looked at me like I was this "perfect" person. "Princess" he would call me. One day I had to come clean and tell him. I couldn't bear living this double life with the one person who, throughout all my heartache, still managed to make my life worth living. What gave me the power to tell him was our strong, solid relationship being built on trust. I couldn't stand the idea that I was keeping this a secret for as long as I had. He handled it like he would handle anything: flawlessly. He was supportive and encouraging and didn't make me feel like I couldn't be trusted again. My family knew, now my husband, and even my best friend. Of course, we all spoke about it when it initially came up, but it's interesting to me: it seemed like it was immediately swept under the rug. I must have been so good at reassuring everyone that it was an issue of the past.

Maybe that's why I always felt like I got away with it.

It seemed like no one knew how to approach it so I would get a lot of vague questions. "Are you okay?" or "Are you feeling good?" Questions that only I would really understand the true meaning behind. As I have always done, I put my poker face on and told them everything was fine. But, was it really?

One Life

My eating disorder was just the beginning of a difficult road ahead.

As the years continued, I stayed the same determined individual. My father always instilled in me to do better than he did: get good grades, go to college, and become a smart, successful career woman. He knew I had it in me and had no doubt that's exactly what I would become. His words and encouragement never left my mind. It wasn't that simple though. The right intentions were there, and I in no way blame my parents, but the pressure of "perfection" came back to me. I was always fearful of disappointing my Dad especially. He had such confidence in me and was always so proud of me for doing well in school. If I received a "B" in school, my parents were pleased, but I on the other hand, would be disappointed in myself. I would lock myself in my room and do whatever I needed to get that "A". It was always self-inflicted pressure, never from them. My Dad always raised me to be a tough, smart woman. My Mom was my best friend in the way that she always reminded me to be confident, have fun in life, and enjoy all that came with being a female.

My Dad was also my hero and best friend. For as long as I remember, he tucked me into bed and scratched my back every night until I fell asleep. My friends would come to hang out with me and stay over just because they really wanted to be hanging out with him. He was just the jokester and funny guy in everyone's life. We were so alike in many ways, but especially work ethic and finances. My Dad was very organized when doing bills. Every Thursday night, we would lie on his bed and do bills together; I was ten years old. He had envelopes for every single bill and credit card. Whenever he made a credit card purchase, he would immediately put the money in the envelope right as the purchase happened. From watching him doing this for so long, I picked up on his habits and responsibilities and have never paid an interest charge on a credit card!

He would leave the house at eight a.m. and return after seven p.m. because he commuted to New York City six days a week, but he always seemed to find a way to be around for the moments that mattered. I can't recall a single soccer game or dance recital when he wasn't there supporting his family. I appreciated it so much, even at a younger age. I recall always wanting to be there for him, too. So I would go with one of my friends every Saturday or Sunday into the city to surprise him at work just so I could spend time with him. It would make his whole day! A couple times I went when I had a fever, and for some reason now that I think of it, I was always sick when I went there. One day I was so sick I fell asleep on one of the beds (it was a high-end furniture store.) Celebrities went there: Brittany Spears, Vanessa Williams, Kelly Ripa, and here I am sleeping on the bed that was for sale. My Dad would walk by with potential buyers and let them know: You can take the bed, but she belongs to me.

My Mom played a huge role in my life, but when it came to decision-making or finances, my Dad was my go-to person. No matter what issue or challenge I came across throughout the years, my Dad constantly told me "you'll find a way" and that's how I made things happen. His faith and support kept me fighting through life's challenges. I could talk to him about anything: boys, money, big purchases, school, etc. He always knew what to say, sometimes nothing other than "Tutu-bean, (our inside joke) you'll find a way."

From the outside in I may have looked like a princess, because I usually got all the things I wanted. The truth is, I worked my ass off for all of those things. I was the first one in my family to attend college. My family was so proud of me for breaking that pattern. I was so close with my parents I refused to go away for college. I couldn't stand the thought of being away from them for four years where I couldn't visit them whenever I wanted to. I chose to attend a local community college where I studied radiography. My Dad told me, "Your first paycheck you can do whatever you want with, but after that you have to save at least sixty percent of it." Of course, I did just that and by twenty-one I was able to buy my first house. I went to sign all the papers by myself, petrified, at twenty-one years old. And so it began, at a time where most would want support I wanted to prove I could do it on my own; they had such confidence in me.

To me, the material items I possessed measured my success.

My life was a list of goals and I was holding the

pen to the "perfect" checklist. Figure competition, check. Dream car, check. Dream home, check.

I made a big profit on my first house, flipped it and sold it. But how could I afford this new house for even more money? My Dad, again, calmed me down. "Tutu-bean, you'll find a way." And at twenty-four years old, I closed on my second house. The continued adrenaline I felt after each big purchase kept me determined to keep chasing anything and everything for money. Until I realized when I had it, I was still so broken and unfulfilled.

I had many great career opportunities. I was always trying to focus on being a successful career woman, being financially stable, and owning property I was proud of. I tried to be a great daughter and an amazing sister. One of the scariest parts of my disorder was that my attention could be elsewhere, (i.e., job, family, friends) and the disorder would still pry its way back into the picture. Unfortunately, even when I wasn't focused on my disorder, it remained focused on me. These are the outcomes of when the disorder snuck back up on me after I thought I had finally overcome it.…

I was sitting in my high school guidance

counselor's office at sixteen years old when I was asked a question that would ultimately change my life forever: *What career do you want to pursue?* Let me pause there. *Who the hell actually knows what they want to do with the rest of their lives at sixteen years old?* I sure didn't! The hardest thing I had to know at that age was which friend I wanted to have over to hang out with me and stay for dinner. I had no *passion* yet for a career. I had no *direction* of where I wanted my life to go. I left that office clueless and came home to talk to my parents and aunt about it. Ultimately, I went into radiography because of that conversation. My aunt had suggested it because that was what she did. She told me all the benefits of the job, most importantly that it paid well and I would have job security. I looked into what the job entails and became a radiographer and MRI Technologist. I intended to join the medical field to help people. Quickly my job turned into an aggressive business. It seemed like the medical field was driven by the pharmaceutical industry and a lot of people preyed on patients for their own personal financial benefits, and I ended up resenting the field.

I continued in radiology for about eight more years before I started searching again to find that passion and true calling. I eventually transitioned to being a patient care coordinator for six years and then I went into management for orthopedic facilities. I jumped around from job to job thinking each new choice I made would make me happier. New jobs offered more money with better hours, but that was really it. I was ultimately doing what I had been doing my whole life: chasing money. The grass must have been greener on the other side because the green coming into my bank account was higher. Unfortunately, no amount of money can bring happiness. I don't believe people truly understand that until they experience it. Bouncing around from job to job I never felt like I was in the right place. To avoid that discomfort, I latched onto my disorder. It was subconscious most times; I would resort to old habits because food was temporarily filling a void. Any time I was sad or stressed or feeling like I didn't enjoy my job, I would come home and eat. I had my family, I was fit, I had a job that was paying me well – what void was I trying to fill? Despite all the jobs, I couldn't find one that moved me in a way to give me purpose. No job made me want to invest my energy or life into its pursuit.

My whole being was focused on success and money rather than passion and purpose. I assumed because I spent years on my education I was stuck in that field. I couldn't fathom the thought of changing careers entirely because it would mean I wasted time and money in school. Plus, what else would I want to do? What else was I good at? I continued jumping around, unsure at the time of what it was that I was truly looking for.

What I didn't know then, was that life could change in the blink of an eye. And no amount of money can change God's plan, and what happened next changed me forever.

I was very naïve to believe my world could be flipped upside down. I went through every day like I was starring in the movie "Groundhog Day" for many, many years, reliving the same day over and over again. I got so caught up living in the day to day I didn't realize how precious life and the people around me were. I thought everything in my life was invincible. On a cold day in March, I was going about my normal routine at work when I discovered the news that left my family and me traumatized and numb.

For months prior, I had been repeatedly asking my Dad to go to the doctor. He had a reoccurring cough that wouldn't go away. He was about to turn 50 and hadn't had a physical in a long time. He said, "I don't need to go to the doctor, I'm healthy, I never get sick." I just needed reassurance he was okay. I wanted him to take a deeper dive than just a typical check-up. A family friend worked for our MD so I asked them to order an EKG and routine blood work for him through my employer. He eventually went and had them done. Results came back normal! However, his cough never went away so we convinced him to get a chest-x-ray. That cold day in March, I put the results up on the imaging viewer and collapsed to the floor. I was hoping that what I saw was wrong, but the Radiologist I worked for confirmed the unimaginable.

Our family doctor then called each of us individually to come home early from work so we could have a family discussion. We all raced home, anxiously awaiting my Dad who had the longest commute. When my mother and sister arrived, I delivered the news to them. We sat crying and shaking as we waited for my Dad thinking, "*How can we deliver this kind of news to the strongest person we know? And who was going to be the one to do it?*" When he finally walked into the living room and looked at all our faces he knew something was terribly wrong. Almost immediately I blurted out, *the doctor called with your test results. Dad, you have cancer.* And it was the first time in my whole life I saw fear in his eyes. We weren't even told yet that it was stage four.

From March on, I was angry at the world. I completely lost faith and blamed God for causing such heartache and pain in my life. My body shut down and I couldn't function the way I had before. I was twenty-five years old and I thought my life was over. There was no coming back from hearing news like that. We all went numb. I kind of remember knowing what *not* to do, but not being able to know what *to do*. When it hits that close to you it's hard to wrap your head around reality and logic. I started questioning everything and everyone. We didn't know any other choice but to put our full trust in doctors, those who were only trained in treating cancer with the conventional treatment methods such as chemotherapy and radiation. The minute Dad started treatment he got weaker and sicker. There was never any good news. It was always one punch in the gut after the other.

The doctors discovered he had two separate primaries, which is rare, located in his kidney and lung. The first step was going in for surgery where they removed a quarter of his kidney. This gave us a little bit of hope thinking the cancer was removed and would be gone forever. What we didn't realize was the other primary, his lung, was the more aggressive one. While focusing on the kidney, the cancer from his lung spread to his mediastinum, and soon after, his brain. This was all within about six months. When the cancer spread to his brain, he was consistently in and out of the hospital; admitted and released, admitted and released. It eventually got to a point where he needed to have brain surgery. I remember that day and felt like I was in the TV show "Grey's Anatomy" because the doctor was explaining exactly what he was going to do for technique in the surgery and we all just froze and became white as a ghost. It was like our souls left us and life just stopped. Hearing that was just as devastating as hearing he had cancer. Again, this surgery was a success and again, we were feeling hopeful. Miraculously (to the doctors), he went back into work shortly after. This was no surprise to us.

Even though the doctors advised against it, he had to continue being who he was.

Although the surgery was a success, after some time he started losing his vision and his demeanor changed. Unfortunately, we had learned the brain cancer came back and had spread to his spine, which eventually left him unable to walk.

I'll never forget one night at home he called me into his bedroom. By some miracle, he got his vision back that day so I made sure to cherish looking into his eyes when we spoke. The words that came out of his mouth next altered the course of my entire life; he said, *"I'm okay to go now because I got to see my family one last time."* It was the first time we let each other see any tears. I don't know how his vision came back, but it seemed like the best miracle that it did. He said to me, *"I have one dying wish."* Those words hit me harder than an eighteen-wheeler. For the first time ever, my Dad acknowledged that he was dying. I swear those words and that reality knocked the wind out of me. In that moment for the first time I finally processed it: my Dad was dying. I leaned closer to hear his wish: *"I'm counting on you to take care of the family."* I said, *"Dad, I'm only twenty-five years old and the youngest, how am I going to do that?"* He locked eyes with mine and said, *"I don't know, but you'll find a way."*

I felt I had the weight of the world on my shoulders, how could I let my father down? If I thought I was only chasing money before this request, it became even more apparent after. Every move I made from this point on was in regards to money.

I spent as many hours possible trying to bring in money. I worked my fulltime job and even added a part time job to generate more income. I would work all week long and train at the gym on the weekends. I was committed to giving my Daddy, my hero, his last wish. This increased hustle and focus continued on for the next few months.

In February, we were all sitting in the dining room for my birthday dinner. My Dad starting speaking irrationally. He became abrasive and angry, verbally aggressive towards us. This brought back memories of behavior that occurred prior to his brain surgery. Because of this we feared the cancer had returned. *How much more could we all take?* Although he was still with us, I felt like I had already lost my Dad. The cancer was stealing his personality even as it was taking his life.

The last thing I wanted to do that night was celebrate. I did not want to leave the house and go out, I just wanted to stay in with my Dad. Being selfless, my Dad insisted I leave the house and go out on my birthday with my friends. That night my Mom called me to tell me she had to call 911 and my Dad was back in the hospital. That was the last night my Dad was ever home.

That year was extremely challenging receiving all the bad news we had, but it was also challenging to have different perspectives on how to handle that bad news. I was ready to quit my job and travel across the world finding alternative treatments to help him find a cure. Unfortunately, he wouldn't even go to another hospital to get a second opinion. It just so happened I worked across the street from the hospital he was admitted to. I would go every single lunch break to sit with him during his chemo treatment.

On one particular day, he yelled, "*Who the hell are you?*" as I walked into the room followed by, "*Where's my daughter, Rinnie?*" Rinnie was my friend. She had grown up with our family. My Dad nicknamed her his "adopted daughter." He had no idea who I was, his actual daughter, but remembered my friend

"Rinnie." That was probably the final turning point where I lost my Dad. His memory of me came and went over the next few days, but even on the days he remembered me I can't say for sure he was completely himself or present. Ironically, the only consistency he had in regards to his memory was related to work. He would talk about having to get back to work often. "*I have to go pay that outstanding invoice in my office. I have to get back to work.*" He couldn't remember his family, but even during his last few weeks, he wouldn't forget about his job.

If I knew then what I know now, I would have inquired more about his diet, seen a nutritionist, went to a holistic wellness doctor – the type I work for now. I would have done something different than just watch him get weaker and sicker as the year went on. I asked the doctor, "How long does he have?" He told me he had six months left. Of course, I went back to work that day hysterical. My boss suggested me taking a leave of absence. Why I didn't, I will never understand.

I guess I am my father's daughter after all.

I spent many days and nights in that hospital room watching my Dad deteriorate and reflecting on our lives together. I recalled his many words of wisdom, jokes, and the more serious conversations. One in particular was my Dad talking about his physical health. *"If I ever have to end up in a wheelchair or get to the point where I can't take care of my family, kill me. I don't want to live if I can't provide for my family."* I was too young and naive to ever take this statement seriously. Now here I was, fifteen years later, watching my Dad struggle to take care of himself. We would have to carry him from room to room, to the bathroom, to bed. As I sit in this hospital room and watch him, I think to myself: this is exactly what he never wanted. But what was I supposed to do? There are different sides to every situation. I wanted to be a little selfish, because I didn't want to see him go. But I also loved him so much I needed to accept his wishes.

My Mom made the decision to move him into hospice. We couldn't bear the thought of him passing away in the house. She quit her job to care for him. She literally wouldn't leave his bedside. Every day I would go visit him. She wouldn't shower or leave ever, not even to eat. She would force me to go home even when I didn't want to. I look back now and still can't understand the superhuman strength she had for dealing with all of this. What was the conversation she was having or what did she say to her high school sweetheart who was lying on his death bed?

I didn't know how to spend all of my time alone (I was not yet married), stressed and heartbroken. I could only wish I was strong enough during that time to resist falling back into old habits. The consistency of my disorder was the only thing I could count on in these unpredictable, emotional days. So, I lived at the gym, (surprise, surprise!) I had told my Mom to only call me if it was "*time.*" And as I was sweating on the elliptical, I received that dreaded call. She quickly hung up after saying, "Ang, come now."

I collapsed on the floor and woke up in the gym owner's arms. When I regained consciousness, I raced to my Dad and my entire extended family was already there. Our nurse, who happened to be our neighbor, had given me a book called *The Five Stages of Death* and the last stage was what to look for in regards to appearance. It was explained during the last stage, his eyes would be open and you would see this yellowish film over them. I looked into his eyes and saw that film. I also had recalled what one of my old boxing coaches told me: when your Dad goes, look out the window because it'll be bright and sunny. So, I looked outside and it was raining and extremely grey and gloomy – so much for that! He would breathe, and then stop breathing, which seemed like an eternity. Every time he did that, we would all hold our breath, too. All along I should have known God had his plan, but in this moment I was praying a miracle would change what was about to come.

My Dad eventually took his last breath as I was lying in bed with him. I looked up out the window: the rain had stopped, and the skies were opening up. And I knew my Dad was making his way to heaven.

When I was growing up he used to joke around that no man in his family lived beyond fifty. He would say *"you girls be nice to me! You'll regret it one day!"* I used to say to him, Dad stop it right now! You will live much longer than that.

After a one-year battle, my Dad, the best Dad in the whole world, passed away at fifty years old on March 10, 2007.

My life spiraled out of control the day he passed away. I tried to push the pain I felt as far back in the memory storage as I could. One big blackout period. Both figuratively and literally.

I started doing things out of character. I never was a big drinker, but I found myself drinking on work nights and it reached a point where I couldn't fall asleep without it. What I thought were challenges and hardships in the past could not come close to the loss of a parent. It was the worst thing to date I have ever been through. I used to pray to not wake up. I actually understood and related to the people who were suicidal, except I was never brave enough to act upon it. And ever since that day my Dad became our angel, there was no joy, no happiness, no light.

One of the darkest times for me was when I found myself in my Mom's kitchen binging. I was eating cereal I didn't even like, eating ice cream out of the container, and anything else that was in arm's reach. My mind must have shut down during the binge and I only regained consciousness when I discovered the whole container was empty. Clearly, my disorder wasn't done with me. My Dad was gone and there I was binging. For every life challenge, binging was my drug, my vice. And even when I thought I was over it, that I had conquered it, I hadn't. Hopelessly, I feared this just might be who I was going to be forever.

Sadly, I accepted that fear. If this was going to be my life, I needed to control it. I knew there would be consequences from my bad habits and I wanted to proactively be one step ahead so I didn't get caught again. Knowing it destroyed your teeth I would immediately brush after; knowing I was losing minerals and vitamins I would replenish my body with a little snack; knowing I would be dehydrated I would chug a bottle of water right after. I did everything I could think of to stay one step ahead.

While the disorder was one vice, I soon found another. I would go out partying with my friends to numb the pain. Truthfully, the only time I felt comforted was when I was at home with my Mom and sister. I didn't want to go out on dates, or meet guys, I wanted to stay as close to my family as I could during this time.

Until one night I went to Lounge 46 with my best friend for her thirtieth birthday. You could imagine the state of mind I was in, trying to have fun for my friend and be out and about, but feeling the constant tugging on my heartstrings over the loss of my Dad. Just when I found myself getting lost in those emotions again, someone shook my arm. "Damion is here and he's walking right towards you!" I used to work with Damion at a sneaker store in the mall when we were sixteen. The last thing I wanted to do was start talking to someone. That night he asked me on a date and I politely declined. However, he would still text me once a week saying something positive just to make me smile. He never gave up. My Mom was actually the one who pushed me into seeing him. She told me, "Dad would not want you sitting here in the house with me every weekend crying. Go out with him!" Luckily for me, Damion stayed persistent and patient, and we finally went out on a few dates.

Eleven months later, he proposed. Eleven months after that, we were married. I have married the best person to come into my life.

A happy end to an otherwise sad story, right?

Wrong!

The first year of marriage is supposed to be the happiest year, filled with love and being preoccupied by the blessings and excitement of this new journey. Well, that was certainly the case for us, and we began trying for a family the first night of our honeymoon. We both wanted to be parents more than anything. We spent the next few months trying to get pregnant. Since my Dad died, Damion did a great job stepping up as the man in the house helping my Mom and grandma whenever they needed anything. He gave everyone a sense of security and peace of mind to have a male figure around to help us girls out. There would be times I would take a backseat and watch what was happening. Damion is so selfless and loving, I knew in my heart that he would always be an amazing father. I felt the pressure though: Would I be a good Mom? I have my own mother, and my older sister who is a mother of three as examples. They set the bar so high that I was afraid I wouldn't be able to live up to either of them. They make it look so easy and effortless. I always have admired them both, but I watched in awe of my sister and loved seeing how beautiful and natural she was with her children. Would I be able to be as successful?

Even with us wanting to be parents as badly as we

did, the best part of being married was the aspects most people take for granted. Having someone to come home to every day after a long day of work, eating meals together and cooking each other's favorite foods, and waking up every morning next to the love of your life. I was this happy when we were engaged, but being married was even more magical for me. I knew my life was finally coming together and I had found the other half to make me whole again. What more could I say? Life was good. We were cruising along in this wonderful life we were creating with each other until it came to a screeching halt. Our "honeymoon phase" was cut shorter than anticipated due to a devastating medical diagnosis.

Who would have thought the results from a simple doctor visit due to headaches would flip our lives this upside down?

We first were sitting in the waiting room for what seemed to be a possible life sentence. When you are that anxious and nervous you try to pass time by reading posters on the wall over and over. Reading magazines that are five months old, looking at the fish tank in the corner. You have no retention though of anything you're reading or watching because your mind is elsewhere. All you are waiting for is for that doctor to call your name and tell you either the best news or the worst. *"Dawes?"*

We both jumped up. We shuffled into the doctor's room and looked at the nurse. "What's the verdict?" we asked. She looked at us both and said, "The doctor will be in shortly." Again, we waited.

Sitting there shaking my leg, it was so quiet you could hear our heart's racing. We were barely breathing, let alone speaking to one another. The doctor finally walked in and we held our breath. She looked at us and recited the most dreaded words you never want to hear, "You have a brain tumor."

She talked for a while after that statement, but again I went into an unconscious state of mind where I couldn't retain anything. I was numb and heartbroken.

After the traumatic emotional journey from losing my Dad to brain cancer, how could we possibly be strong enough for this? Immediately we started treatment and medication and watched the symptoms start fading away. The specialist cautioned us that if the symptoms came back after treatment, surgery would be needed. Unfortunately, the symptoms did indeed come back, and we didn't know what to do. Like in every situation when someone gets stressed: you either need one of two things: a drink or a getaway. And for this kind of news, a drink alone would not help. So, we decided to take the first flight to Mexico to try to escape the inescapable. We needed some time to pretend what was happening at home could stay there. We wanted to forget the pain for a little while and regain our strength and faith for what we knew would be a difficult time when we returned home. While we were away, we pondered if we weren't getting pregnant because of this diagnosis. After gaining some courage when we were home, we asked the doctors if this were true. Heartbreakingly, the doctors told us it could be. While some couples would fall apart or go into a dark place after receiving news like this, our marriage grew stronger and we grew closer to one another. Things that stressed me out about him were no longer issues. I found myself not wanting to do anything without him. I was usually independent but now I wanted to always have him by my side. I was more conscious of his feelings and considered his opinions. We focused on being ourselves: goofy, silly, and trying to always laugh. We started going to church together because we both knew how crucial it was to have strong faith at this time.

The struggles we faced together were difficult and draining, both emotionally and financially, but the important factor was that we were always in this together.

The first day back from our getaway we found a specialist able to provide a second opinion. We found a team of doctors specializing in that type of tumor. Without giving any advice or opinion, they wanted us to repeat the MRI scan with their team.

Again, the waiting period...

It took some time to get the results, but when we finally had them we found ourselves yet again sitting in a waiting room anticipating our fate.

This time, the doctor visit ended a little differently. A miracle seemed to be happening: we were told there was a misdiagnosis. "There is no tumor, it was only a shadow." However, they advised us to come back in six months for a reevaluation. Feeling so shocked yet relieved, we couldn't even come up with questions to inquire about the misdiagnosis.

Obviously feeling blessed, we immediately tried to return to our lives before this nightmare. The only thing that had changed between us was that we had even more respect, love, and faith in our marriage and relationship.

After some time had passed, the symptoms unfortunately came back. Initially I was in denial and didn't want to accept that these symptoms were anything but fabricated in my head. We were told it was a shadow! Damion finally convinced me we needed to seek a third opinion.

YET AGAIN, we were sitting in a doctor's office waiting room.

We were brought back to a challenging place when that new specialist told us the original diagnosis still stood; it was in fact a tumor.

Based on size, shape, location and specific blood work, the doctor assured us it was benign and we had no reason to operate or treat it. We only had to monitor the symptoms and semi-annually go in for a MRI to make sure the size and appearance hadn't changed. If any symptoms appeared we were to contact him immediately.

Of course I was ecstatic, but I almost couldn't believe it. It was hard for me to trust anyone at that point. I felt like a ping-pong ball, going back and forth with all the contradictory information. It was hard to know how long this feeling of relief would last. Years of wasted emotions, hospital visits, and money all for uncertainty.

Because of this emotional roller coaster, we felt sick to our stomachs. We still had the previous doctor's words echoing in our heads: "*I want you to believe in me and trust me when I tell you: you have nothing to worry about.*" We felt confused and hurt; whom could we trust if not the most advanced in the field? We felt so angry and frustrated not knowing who to turn to or who was really in our corner. We wanted to take matters into our own hands after so many misdiagnoses. We changed our diets, how we were exercising, what we were putting into our bodies. We wanted to make sure the "out of sight, out of mind" phrase held water. If you keep being told you have a brain tumor, all of a sudden you have headaches. If your vision starts getting blurry, you panic that the tumor is getting worse. Instead, we just needed glasses.

Being consumed by so many different emotions, it was easy to forget all the other goals and dreams we had as a married couple. Because we spent so much time over the course of a year focusing on the tumor, we put becoming parents on the back burner.

With the tumor being benign, we were able to focus more of our energy and attention on becoming pregnant. We had to accept the fact that after all we had been through, the tumor was no longer a reason for infertility.

Starting a family with each other became that much more meaningful to both of us. We wanted to be able to love something more than just ourselves. To have someone look up to us to love and respect us, and to solely be responsible to raise a child – we don't realize how self-consumed and selfish we are until we get to the point where we have another life in our hands. I wanted to experience all of the joys and pains that come with child bearing.

When I was younger I never wanted to get married and have kids: I wanted the career and independence. Previously, life was always about me, but I was never truly fulfilled. It was only until I met my husband that I started opening up to the idea that a family was the last piece to the puzzle to mend my damaged heart.

Unfortunately, since we were so consumed we didn't realize time was flying by us. It was a full year and still no baby. Taking the focus off of the tumor we tried to understand what was happening with conceiving. Doctors originally thought we weren't getting pregnant because the hormones were being compromised due to the tumor's location. We both agreed that if we had to choose between being together and healthy versus having a child we would choose us, first and always. As painful as it was to imagine a life with no children of our own, the thought of one of us not being here in this world was just too difficult to bear.

When you are told you can't have or do something, that's when you realize how badly you truly want it. You take it all for granted until someone says, "I'm sorry, I just don't think it's possible for you guys." It's a definitive punch in the gut. It's honestly hard to even put into words: the thought of never having a baby is simply devastating.

In my life, on a stress level from one to ten I was probably at a 100. As if the health issues weren't stressful enough, my current job was making matters worse. I was stuck in a job that gave me no purpose. I was there to collect a paycheck. I had no passion or motivation to do anything else within the company. At the time, we didn't realize how stress and anxiety could impact the success of becoming pregnant. I did everything I could to try to find peace within my life, myself, and the events that were occurring. I left that job and tried to find another one to hopefully ease my troubles financially and mentally.

Yet again, my husband proves to be the hero. His words to me were, "We can sell the house, give up everything we have just so you don't have to be in that environment anymore. After all, your health and well-being is the most important to me." He gave me his blessing to leave my job and follow my heart to do what makes me happy. But I wasn't sure what that was. I had received my board certification to be a holistic health coach a few years back. I wanted my clients to feel great about themselves and embrace the amazing self-healing machines our bodies truly are. My family told me, "This is what you're meant to do. You have a gift with helping people." However, it wasn't easy for me to continue being a coach without wondering if I was sounding or coming across as hypocritical. I was telling my clients to be positive, have faith, and trust our bodies to self-heal and those were some of the areas that were breaking down in my own life. I started feeling like I couldn't coach anymore, because it was affecting my life so much. I felt I had to look or act a certain part. The more I helped others the more I felt like they were judging me. How do you help someone piece their puzzle together when you have your own missing pieces? Once again, my disorder found it's way back into my life.

I spent the next few months truly prioritizing my well-being. I needed to eliminate any tangible reason for possible infertility whether that was from work stress, finances, or my disorder. I really focused on centering myself to find peace and bliss so I could say I did everything within my power to achieve a successful pregnancy.

We continued trying, but we still weren't getting pregnant. We were running out of reasons. It seemed like we were hitting dead ends.

After many failed conclusions, we came to a decision together to accept that we were not getting pregnant the traditional way and began our journey with fertility specialists and treatments.

Over the next eight years, we visited four different fertility clinics, had eight procedures, and four miscarriages.

Our strength and faith were greatly tested over those eight years. Some days I would take my anger and frustration out on him when I was feeling my weakest, which usually was during the daily injections. He would also repeatedly ask me if there's anything he could do to help, which made me very irritated and anxious. I just wanted to be left alone.

I hated the way I treated him during those times, but I was so vulnerable and raw I didn't know how else to respond to all of this. I became very short-tempered and angry from being exhausted all the time. Our medical insurance didn't have fertility benefits, so the financial stress was icing on the cake. The bills poured in quicker than they could even be opened. I could understand how marriages fall apart during this grueling process, but luckily ours grew stronger.

I couldn't fathom doing this with any other man by my side. If I didn't have my husband who is as strong, loyal, and compassionate as he is, I would have never been able to go through with all of it. I thank God every day for his commitment and strength to this marriage and to me.

Each morning I had to take injections at the same time, I would wake up at 4:45 a.m. for my husband to do the injection. And on top of that, three to four days a week I had to drive forty minutes away for monitoring through blood work and ultrasound. They would open at six a.m., but if I got there any later than 5:30 a.m. the line would be around the corner. And then I would have to drive back home and start my day; after all I still had a fulltime job. My ten to twelve hour long days would make me even more exhausted. I would crawl through my front door at the end of every night.

Since I believe in holistic wellness and rarely used medication I was doing the opposite of what I believed in, which really frustrated me. I had no idea what was the purpose of each of the different prescriptions I was required to take. All I did know was that my hormones were completely out of balance. I became short tempered and cranky. It was like I hated the world. I began to have fear for things I never feared, anger towards women who were pregnant or already had children. I would question myself all the time: I was the one who worked out and was healthy. Everything you should do to get pregnant I did, and it meant nothing. I started questioning if I did not deserve to be a mother. Soon after all aspects of my life began collapsing like dominos. And if you've ever watched dominos fall; you know how hard it is to stop the momentum once it has started.

After some time had passed my body struggled to continue its normal routine. Walking became difficult and at times unbearable. Little did I know we were injecting into my sciatic nerve.

I became hyper stimulated and very swollen. The doctor advised me that I was no longer able to work out, which affected me in more than one way. Working out was my stress reliever in life; it was also my go-to vice when I was stressed and sad. I also couldn't stand the fact that I was putting on weight. I consistently felt frustrated and insecure about how I looked, but my husband would always assure me that I still looked "hot" and that he loved my body. This is another example of how my eating disorder stayed focused on me when I thought I was not focused on it. My mind was consistently being distracted with the changes that were happening with my body, rather than focusing on the end result of becoming a mother.

Our sex life was also affected. While sex might have been initiated due to love and passion, the focus during each encounter shifted to an unspoken pressure that nether one of us would address. The elephant in the room during sex was always the question: Are we going to get pregnant?

We had a full Excel spreadsheet of the medicine I had to take during this process. It was challenging for me to have such a dramatic lifestyle flip. I went from being the person who wouldn't even take an Advil when I had a headache, to taking multiple pills throughout the day. I also had to do injections and sometimes that was multiple times a day as well. On top of all of that, needles were my biggest fear ever since I was little. When it was time to do an injection, the anxiety I felt (I can't find a synonym that makes anxiety a strong enough description) was unbearable. Before every injection Damion would put on country music. It was my favorite genre and his least favorite. He would even make me start to sing along before the injections to make sure I was in my happy place. After the injection he would get a warm cloth and rub it on me for fifteen minutes to lessen the pain and inflammation. That is another example why Damion went above and beyond for me: to comfort me through my biggest fear.

Some nights I would get home from work really late and he would be waiting for me at the door to carry in all my things. He would immediately start doing all my dishes from the day, and make tea for me just so I could wash up, and get ready for the nightly injection. He wouldn't go out with his friends on the weekends because he didn't want to leave me at home alone. He would always repeat: "We are in this together." He would text me something positive every day from work. I never wanted to fall asleep without him so he would lay with me until I did and then he would carefully get up and go watch his shows on TV.

One of the last doctors we went to said they've never seen a stronger couple. Damion was, is, and will always be my backbone.

People always say, "If something's not meant to be, it won't happen, no matter how badly you want it to." We wanted to become parents more than anything, but true to the phrase, no matter how badly we wanted that, it just wasn't happening. We later found out the two places we were doing treatments weren't testing us for all of the things we could have been tested for. We did six procedures at the first two facilities and I didn't feel comfortable anymore and begged my husband to try somewhere new. Again, the story of our lives, we wanted another opinion. Two of my friends went to a different facility and were successful, so we thought we should give it a try. It wasn't until the third and final facility where the tests showed how much more there was to actually consider. Even with all of those tests, they all came back negative. We were this medical mystery the doctors just couldn't figure out. Since there was no documented reason why we couldn't get pregnant, we all had faith to believe it would eventually happen.

Switching facilities was a lot riskier than simply meeting a new doctor. That's what truly kept us at the facilities longer than we wanted to be at. We had a traumatizing experience while transferring between facility one and two.

We had four remaining frozen embryos that

needed to be transferred and we decided to pick them up ourselves to ensure there was no mishandling. My doctor reiterated that he didn't know the quality of the embryos and I would have to undergo the prep for a transfer (which entailed more drugs and needles) and that he wouldn't know until the day of the procedure when the embryos thawed. That meant there was a chance I went through all of this for nothing because we wouldn't know the viability of the embryos.

The morning of the procedure the doctor called and said three out of the four straws were broken. Straws are what hold the embryo in place. Think of a toothpick and a grape, the grape is the embryo and the toothpick is the straw. The grape will fall off and drop to the floor if the toothpick doesn't exist. Chances are the embryos were lost and floating around in the nitrogen water. (A liquid that is stable and makes it a good medium for storing frozen cells or tissues)

I repeatedly asked myself if I personally carried the tanks from one facility to another, how could this have happened? The current embryologist even stated they had never seen this outcome from a transfer. There were two possibilities: one, they were mishandled in the technique of getting them ready for transportation. Or two, the current embryologist mishandled them in extracting them from the nitrogen tank. Either way I knew I would never know the real reason.

Now we only had one embryo remaining with no idea of the quality. We took a chance and implanted the embryo, which was actually against the doctor's medical opinion. He believed we should be starting fresh and not implanting that last remaining embryo. The simple reason was, he didn't know the quality and specifics, as he did not work for the facility that did the initial egg retrieval.

The retrieval process is one of the most painful aspects of IVF. I had to take pills, injections, and monitor everything happening in my body. It took a huge toll on me, both physically and emotionally. And in my mind, these embryos were my children. It isn't easy to give up and just say "Discard it, dispose of it. We'll start with a new batch." I tried to see the glass as half full, not half empty. And I wasn't ready to dispose of any hope, opportunity, or possibility that the embryo was going to give my husband and I a baby.

We found ourselves yet again, sitting and waiting for that phone call with the results from the blood work to determine if the procedure was a success.

Another heartbreaking call, another failed procedure.

Here we go again, starting over. Again, I'm trying to figure out how to stay positive in my world, which was filled with so much negativity.

Once more, I am repeatedly telling myself to "Let Go and Let God." I hoped that one-day I would whole-heartedly do just that. I wanted to believe so bad, but deep down inside I was beginning to lose faith.

The end result, throughout all the trials and tribulations, I learned: do your homework. Because we were naïve to infertility we didn't know what to expect. We didn't know what questions to ask, or what the consequences of certain actions could be. If we could give any advice, it would be to do your research. Understand the material and subject matter enough to be an expert. Also become the expert when it comes to your health and body. Don't go into any procedures blindly, or simply put your full trust in others. Challenge yourself to leave your comfort zone and seek others that have been through the same experience. It was a very difficult time for my husband and me and it seemed like it was never-ending.

Although, I truly believe God needed me to go through those challenges in my life. I don't think I would be the person I am today, or will be in the future, if I didn't go through those life experiences. Every challenge presented to me was an opportunity for me to overcome them. And every time I overcame something, my confidence grew and I became stronger. I realized that after my fifth miscarriage. It didn't hurt any less, but I was able to find peace knowing that God already had a plan.

Throughout my life I kept trying to find the answers to all of life's heartache and bad news. What I discovered was that I wasn't going to have all of the answers to everything. Sometimes life is just shitty and there's no good reason at all. What I've learned along the way was: you don't need all of the answers you only need one. Once I was able to let go of that expectation, I was finally able to begin the healing process.

And the one thing I realized most (better late

than never):

> *"Getting over a painful experience is much like crossing monkey bars. You have to let go at some point in order to move forward."* (C. S. Lewis)

Photo credit: Stolen Moments Photography

Angela Dawes and Vanessa Sullivan

One Answer

There are many who are in their own dark place, currently, previously, or even in the days ahead. Know that you are not alone. Whether it's an eating disorder, infertility, a loss of a parent, or any other challenge- you are not alone.

Unfortunately, I had to hit an all-time low before I realized that what I was doing was simply not the answer. I was still deeply depressed (often suicidal), helpless, and hopeless. It became very frustrating when so many specialists couldn't provide me with any answers, but continued to flood my body with medication.

Until the day I was finally led to Dr. Roger Sahoury, a Chiropractic Neurologist at Above and Beyond Holistic Wellness Center. He gave me hope and knowledge that no one else did. The initial consultation was extremely thorough and included a complete Nervous System Scan and Biostructual X-rays; both of which I never had before. Dr. Roger explained that the body has the innate intelligence to heal itself, if there's no interference. My scan showed that I had severe interference in my nerves and that my cervical spine had a reverse curve, preventing life flow to my brain and major organs. I took a leap of faith and immediately went under corrective care treatments. After a few months under care I had hope, and within one year I started to regain my life back. I was off all my medications; he had healed me both emotionally and physically.

Beneath all my pain and suffering, Dr. Roger saw my potential and always believed in me. When I wanted to give up on myself, he never did. I never met someone who has more heart, passion and mission to save lives. Without any doubt he has been my angel, my healer, and I'm grateful that I was led to him.

I too will be growing and changing in the many years to come. I've come to realize that "perfection" does not exist- so I need to stop striving for it. And seeking help and support is critical.

*"Be strong enough to stand
alone, smart enough to know
when you need help, and
brave enough to ask for
it." (Ziad K. Abdelnour)*

Throughout the years I had my ups and downs especially recovering from my eating disorder. Because there were many times I couldn't save myself I felt desperate to try to save others. Any time a situation came up where I could extend a helping hand to someone in need, I jumped on the opportunity.

It just so happens a woman I knew had a fifteen-year-old daughter who was suffering from an eating disorder as well.

I tried to reason with her over these terrible thoughts that come from the disorder. I recall all those conversations on a regular basis, and my heart still aches when I remember how painful some of them were. As a woman it's hard to have this pressure of "perfection" in your life, but watching young, innocent girls dealing with this disorder is unbearable.

Her parents called me one day after their daughter had a really emotional week. I went by the house and tried to talk to her face to face and understand what was making her binge and purge. Throughout our discussion, she kept repeating that she thought she was fat. She was disgusted with how she looked. I couldn't believe the words she was saying, because she was so beautiful. I immediately felt like I was talking to a younger version of myself. I wanted to be open and raw with her, in hopes that the next question I would ask could be the turning point in her recovery. I wanted her to see that there was so much more in life to be grateful for.

I remember asking her, "If I could grant you one wish- what would you wish for?"

Without hesitation, she replied, "To have long thin legs like a runway model."

I was shocked! Of all things to wish for, she chose that? Even still, I snapped my fingers and said, "Your wish is granted! You now have the legs you want. Fine. Done. But ... tomorrow you wake up and have been diagnosed with stage four cancer. You eventually become blind, than paralyzed. WHAT ARE THOSE LEGS WORTH NOW?"

As we gazed at one another with tears slowly

rolling down our cheeks, she whispered "Everything."

I was left speechless trying to find the right words to say. I finally said to her: "That story was about my father. He did not have the choice to be healthy. Cancer took that from him. You and I are choosing to destroy our bodies. We do have a choice; we can do better; we can heal!

In that very moment, a warm rush came over me. I knew my Dad was there with me, speaking through me.

Stolen Moments Photography

I believe I was chosen to be the voice, so she could have her breakthrough. But little did I know, I would have my very own. And in that moment, I made the decision to honor my body and myself. Finally, that was the end to a very long battle of bulimia, but the beginning to a whole new healthy me!

I've learned achieving health should be a lifelong journey not only for a specific event. Even though I may have a wedding coming up or it's just the summertime, health should be my priority regardless.

Although the fitness industry wasn't the right lifestyle for me, there are those in the industry who have made that their lifestyle and trained successfully while remaining healthy. The important difference between those and others is acknowledging how critical it is to understand what's actually healthy and required for our body. Regardless of the sport we're in, there are ways to train and excel. In my personal opinion, balance is what a lot of people lack. Instead of panicking and rushing to lose weight, or get shredded (lean muscle mass) and trying to crash diet, it's about training all year long. We must commit to a healthy diet and exercise throughout all seasons, not just the one we're competing in. That doesn't mean never have a reward meal or never take the day off from working out, but finding that blissful balance. Knowing that health is about the big picture: after all, our body is our temple to live in. We cannot trade it in for a younger model when we've overworked it or damaged it.

Yesterday is gone; all we have is right now. I said goodbye to where I've been and left my shadows behind me. I trusted, regained faith and knew there was hope in front of me.

I challenge you: let your story play out, and just have some faith. Life is unpredictable, and it might not go as we plan. It may catch us off guard when we least expect it, but we can't give up. Our miracle can happen; we can find our purpose, and our "ah-ha!" Moment. When I wake up in the morning and have another chance to breathe that is the miracle. And God is saying I am giving you another opportunity to thrive. Every day I am alive that in itself is something to celebrate.

Joseph Campbell once said,

> *"We have to let go of the life we have planned . . .. to accept the one that is waiting for us."*

Without even realizing it, our struggles in life prepare us for what is coming next.

I have discovered something that is bigger than myself, something that gives me a whole new outlook on life. I've learned that what's broken can be mended. What hurts can be healed. And no matter how dark it gets, the sun is going to rise again. Sometimes we need to give our frustrations over to God and accept the things we cannot change. My favorite quote is the serenity prayer:

> *"God grant me the serenity*
> *to accept the things I cannot*
> *change, the courage to change*
> *the things I can, and the*
> *wisdom to know the difference."*
> *(Reinhold Niebuhr)*

Along my journey I was able to discover what it would take to live a happy life. Twenty years ago if you were to ask me, "What does happiness mean to you?" I would respond with "Financial success!" Here I am, my journey still evolving, but I do know how to answer that question correctly now. I have finally discovered *the answer*.

> *Seek out your true passion by*
> *discovering your purpose.*

Take a second to absorb that.

Take another one.

Wait… one more.

So how did I discover my purpose? By simply realizing what makes me happy; what brings me joy; what excites me. I allowed life to happen and take place. I watched my life unfold. Loosen the reigns and lose control over every situation. I rolled with the punches. There is something special and unique about you, something that defines you. You have a calling, a purpose in life! Everybody has something great they are destined to do, so it is possible to do what you love and also thrive.

How to lead you to your "*one answer*":

When you do what you love, you will always find inspiration. The goal is to find true happiness and live a fulfilled life. The answer is right in front of you; you just have to embrace it. The answer will give you the inspiration and courage to find what makes you happy. I challenge you: take a piece of paper and write down what brings you happiness. You have to find out what will bring you happiness before you can find out what will lead you or get you there.

Here are some questions that may stimulate your mind. These questions will challenge you to think outside of your norm, to dream a little bit bigger, and try to understand what really can make you happy.

1. If you didn't need to worry about a paycheck, what job would you pursue because you are simply intrigued in the work?

2. If you had time, freedom, and no routine schedule, what would you spend your time doing?

3. Is there something that you do, or somewhere that you go, when you want to escape the chaotic and stressful world we often live in?

Now if you're looking for guidance to those answers, here's my own discovery. Our primary source of happiness may be the same whether it comes from our job, our hobbies, or where we would escape to if we need a break. On the other hand, some prefer to separate the three. If our work isn't bringing us happiness, there are other opportunities out there. We shouldn't feel stuck. Life is too short to be doing something we don't enjoy. We have the ability to make these types of changes in our life. Let's take control over the things we actually can control and write our own destiny.

Life is meant to be lived! We get so caught up in the day-to-day routines, that we forget to let loose and have some fun.

I have a routine, every part of the day I am focusing on doing something that will keep me from slipping back into old, bad habits. When I'm around people and in public I am probably at an eight on the strength scale of one to ten. At home, by myself, I'm more around a five. And I truly do feel like I found my passion and happiness in life. Even when you have found your true calling and your "one answer" that doesn't mean you're "perfect." Remember: there's no such thing. Finding your happiness and passion means you found the missing links in your heart's puzzle that completes you. You found your purpose in this world, on how to make it a better place by giving back to your community, the planet, your family, or sometimes even just yourself. Finding your answer means you might be at a five on the strength scale, but you know that that's okay. You might fall apart some days, and be sad other days, but it's okay. Because overall, life is good. You're good. You're in a good place and no bad news can take that away from you.

However …

Sometimes life just sucks. And you're not good. And you're not in a good place, and bad news put you there.

For when that happens, I have a few different strategies that helped me cope with my disorder and push through the days that were too difficult. One huge part of my recovery was sticky notes. I used to put them on the inside lid of the toilet bowl, for example: "You are stronger than this!" I would have to remind myself I only have one body, a temple if you will, sacred and beautiful and I was obligated to take care of it. Your body is your safe zone, and as the famous words of Eleanor Roosevelt,

> *"No one can make you feel*
> *inferior without your consent."*

The trouble was, most of my life it was me making myself feel inferior. No one else! So this is where the concept of *Safe Words* derived.

I first thought of all the things in the world that made me feel happy and at peace. I narrowed them down to my favorite word of all: BELLA. This is the name of my first niece. There is not one negative thought when I think of her. Not only was she the first child in our family, she is also my Goddaughter. Her name means beautiful, the word I was so often trying to convince myself that I am.

Breathe
Empower
Let Go
Laugh
Accept

Now that I've chosen my Safe Word, I created a set of instructions to instantaneously change my mindset when I feel I'm beginning to spiral out of control. If you can't think of a Safe Word, please feel free to use mine. No matter what Safe Word you have, or where it originated, the power of the word is ultimately dependent on your belief of the process. Here's my breakdown:

Breathe – Take slow, deep belly breaths; repeat, "this too shall pass."

Empower – Repeat to yourself a confident phrase such as, "I am enough." "I am beautiful."

Let Go – Let go of any feeling that is crippling you. Release them all. Don't overanalyze or stress.

Laugh – Laugh it off. Think of your favorite funny memory; actually start laughing out loud for no reason at all, however it comes, just laugh.

Accept – Accept yourself. Let this process come full circle. Accept your flaws and rise above them.

You can have an unlimited number of Safe Words. I personally have two. My first Safe Word did not seem as fitting when I was going through other heartaches, so I created another one. My goofball of a sister, who I think is the funniest person in the world, would like to embarrass me when we were growing up. When we were young and would be in a store, she would chase after me screaming "Balls!" because it would embarrass me and make her laugh. To this day the word makes me crack up! So, I made it into my next Safe Word. BALLS. (Breathe, Accept, Let Go, Laugh, Self-Forgive) The breakdown might be similar, but the Safe Word you choose is ultimately dependent on your current situation.

Breathe
Accept
Let Go
Laugh
Self-Forgive

I'm inserting the Safe Word as a reminder that no matter where you are in your life, in your school day, in your marriage, in your own journey, you can pause and regroup to gain composure. You CAN be in control.

And then you can press play and continue on, fighting and battling to remain strong. You have to recharge and regroup because you have no idea what lies ahead.

The greatest challenge in life is accepting who you are, realizing what makes you happy, discovering what's important, and disregarding everything else.

"Perfection" doesn't exist. We all have a different definition of "perfect" in our mind. And I can tell you from experience, most of those definitions are wrong. The closest traits of "perfect" is making many mistakes and still trying; falling down and getting back up; understanding that life isn't easy and often not fair. Having these traits and knowing everything can go utterly wrong, but still loving yourself through those times- that is the only definition of "perfect" I'll accept.

I soon realized that it's not about finding your happy ending; it's about the journey.

Telling my journey and knowing it's not over. It doesn't end with college, or marriage, or a career, or your kids; your story doesn't ever stop evolving. Every day you turn the page to your own story and you choose how to make it end. However, sometimes you can't control the outcome and sometimes you can't control the news you receive.

While I was writing this book my husband and I found out that we were pregnant again. We were overjoyed and beyond blessed.

After two and half months, I found out I lost the baby. I was completely devastated. My heart shattered thinking how unfair life is. I wondered, "Why does this keep happening to me?" I gave myself the time I needed to cry every drop of water out of my body, and then I put my big girl pants on. My journey isn't over because another pregnancy was. Although my heart will forever be broken for this baby and all of the babies I lost, I can't let their loss define who I am. There is still more for me to accomplish out in the world, and if I fall victim and let the heartbreak consume me, I'll never be able to find out what that is.

You may never get the answers you are searching for. Throughout the whole fertility process, I was desperate to know why I kept having miscarriages. The doctors response was simply stated as, "mystery infertility". Seriously? It feels that this has been my life story: never a concrete diagnosis.

You can either live in the unknown where you keep questioning everything, or you can accept the unknown, and stop trying to control the uncontrollable. This is THE HARDEST LESSON. Sometimes I wonder if I would have found my true purpose if I had been blessed with children at those times. I learned that I needed to feel whole again before I could heal. I needed to feel empowered before I could gain strength. To feel love before I could love a child of my own.

Looking back now, was I even capable of loving a child when I didn't love myself? Although I am now healed of my eating disorder, I still have weak moments when challenges arise. I never act upon them, but the thoughts linger. I've come to place where I love and respect my body and myself. Once I was able to resolve the internal conflicts, I was able to able to fully appreciate the external blessings around me.

Through all my life's events, I have discovered the **biggest blessing** in all of this: my husband, Damion. I had to have faith and know that God has His plan for me and I may not understand it now, or have understood it then, or even agree with it, but it is God's plan. Discovering this has also allowed Damion and I to build the foundation of trust, communication and respect. To me, these are the most important components of relationships that others don't focus enough time and energy on building. I wouldn't take back us going through these challenges because we grew closer to one another. Would we have gotten the chance to make our relationship bulletproof if we got married and had kids right away? We will never know, but if I thought our relationship was solid before all the heartache, it's cement now. My mindset changed with my marriage to Damion. I saw broken; he saw blessed. I lost faith; he helped me to believe. If I ever find myself getting caught up in moments of frustration, I put my full trust in God and know he has a plan for me.

I believe in God so that's whom I reference when I reflect on my own life's path. There is a path, but you're going to go off-roading, A LOT. You have to stay in the mindset that you don't have control over most of life's events. You have to stay in the mindset that "perfection" doesn't exist. Life is going to pull the rug from under you some days. It's critical to stay composed and have faith that it's all going to work out in the end.

*"Sometimes God lets you hit
rock bottom so that you will
discover that he is the rock at
the bottom." (Tony Evans)*

Out of all that has happened to me, I am reminded that I am who I am because of those moments. And not only living through those moments, but surviving through them as well.

We live in an "instant world" today that is also streamed for everyone else to see; a society that needs to know everything, quicker and faster. On a daily basis we are bombarded with impossibly "perfect" images that have been altered by airbrushing or digitally manipulated. There are free photo-editing apps that can instantaneously make the photo look different. We are distracted with instant gratification and with information that seems so easy. There are people posting on social media getting shared thousands of times, with jaw dropping graphic design and videos that are produced so flawlessly. What we see is the finished product, not the behind the scenes raw version.

You never know someone's story from how they look on the outside. If you battle an eating disorder like I did, there is an unspoken pressure to look a certain way. If you are an alcoholic, there is a bar on every street corner. If you're overweight, there's an unhealthy fast food place every mile. Whatever battle you are facing, there is constant temptation surrounding you. However, you have a choice. Just because temptation is in front of you doesn't mean you should give in. Sometimes the hardest choice and the right choice is often the same.

Life is heavily influenced by our attitude. Every day we make a decision to either embrace happiness or give into sadness. The choice is up to us. Pain can either break us down or build us up; it's all about perspective. We can choose to see only heartache and misery, or we can see the necessary parts of life we don't have control over. It is easy to give up and wallow in self-pity, but it takes courage to move forward and build a new life in the face of tragedy. All the strength we need is inside of us.

We are conditioned to focus on the negative versus the positive. We have to reprogram ourselves to "focus on what's going right in the moment, rather than what's going wrong." (Dr. Roger Sahoury)

I was told by many how negative emotions such

as fear, resentment, and anger can lead to illness or disease. I knew if I wanted to heal and move forward I had to make a decision … I had to let go. I had to release all the toxic build up inside of me so I could make room for healing to occur. Healing doesn't mean the damage never existed. It means the damage no longer consumes us. The things we believe in and focus on will always have power over us. If you focus on good things they will happen, or, you can choose to fear the unknown. Once we realize that fear is a state of mind, we can choose to face our fears. I wanted to take a negative situation and form a positive bigger picture. For instance, when I injured my back, I couldn't work out for months. Of course, I was frustrated and devastated at the thought of not working out for that long. However, I took a step back from the situation and reminded myself to see the bigger picture: I could still walk! A more difficult example, and one I was only able to grasp until recently, was the loss of my Dad. That pain and heartache won't ever go away, but the blessing is that I still have my incredible mother.

Alongside reprogramming our minds to see the positive rather than the negative, it is also important to look forward rather than behind. If you can't visualize a future for yourself, how can you expect to move out of the past? While it might be challenging to break old habits, the goal is to wake up a different person than you were the day before. When you change the way you look at things, the things you look at change.

> *"I am not what happened to me. I am what I choose to become." (Carl Jung)*

I realize the truth now that I didn't then: I needed to go through those challenges in order to get to the place that I am today. The dark moments will come. You will feel empty and all out of hope. Sometimes in order to discover our true purpose we need to face the darkest moments that leave us broken and helpless. But it is in those moments that we discover our true strengths that will carry us through those dark tunnels.

> *"You cannot control all the events that happen to you, but you can decide not to be reduced by them." (Maya Angelou)*

Let the healing begin! Remember:

The only way to protect us from the dangers in this ever-changing world is to change along with it.

Change the way you respond to challenges. You must find a way to cope. It is less about managing stress and more about how you interact with it. Instead of trying to fight against the emotions, try to understand them. Greet negativity with a new perspective.

> *"Your world is not falling apart, it's falling into place." ~ Casting Crowns*

One Body, *One* Life, *One* Answer.

One Body: Take care of yourself both physically and emotionally. You have one body and one mind: embrace it, love it, and respect it!

One Life: Value life and how precious it is. You are gifted only one life and you and/or your loved ones are not guaranteed tomorrow.

One Answer: Seek out your true passion by discovering your purpose.

When you embrace the three "*Ones*" your mind, body, and soul will discover unconditional happiness.

> *"When I look back on my life, I see pain, mistakes and heartache. When I look in the mirror, I see strength, learned lessons, and pride in myself." (Unknown)*

I am amazed on how much I've learned. I believe God placed me on this path because I needed to learn lessons and experience all that I did. I was finally able to bring the three "*Ones*" together full circle. I've grown tremendously over the years and I am so proud that I am able to step back from every situation and reflect on it. The good, the bad, the raw. The most valuable lesson for me was learning the true definition of strength. As difficult as my journey has been, I value those lessons immensely. Money isn't important, no matter how much you think it will help change your life I can tell you from my experience: money alone won't bring you happiness. This journey has showed me what life is truly about: that one must determine one's proper priorities, that the heartaches are just as important as the celebrations, and that love and strength really does conquer all.

Stolen Moments Photography

Angela Dawes and Vanessa Sullivan

Letter to my Mom:

There's nothing more you could have ever done or said. I needed to go through each and every challenge to become who I am today. Since Daddy left to be our angel, you have stepped up and been the calm during my storms. When I was weak, you gave me strength. When I was insecure, you gave me confidence. When I needed answers to the unimaginable, you stayed truthful and showed me love. You've carried me through, when I was convinced I couldn't go on. Thank you for holding me while I cried and promising me that tomorrow would be a better day. You have always been my support system and believed in me. You taught me that you could rise above your cir-cumstances and to never give up on my dreams. You're my inspiration and the most amazing Mom a girl could ever dream of having. Thank you for all that you do, I love you!

Through *pain* I found *purpose*.

Through *faith* I found *peace*.

Follow me as I continue to share my

healing journey from *"Broken to Blessed."*

www.purposeofmine.com

www.facebook.com/angelamdawes

www.instagram.com/purposeofmine

www.instagram/com/brokentoblessed_

Angela Dawes and Vanessa Sullivan